VOICES OVER WATER

D. Nurkse lives in Brooklyn, New York. His parents fled Nazi
Europe during World War Two. He has published nine books
of poetry, most recently *Burnt Island* (2003) and *The Border
Kingdom* (2008); he has also written on human rights issues
and worked with Amnesty International USA.

'I can't praise D. Nurkse's poems enough. I go to them to
hear "the still sad music of humanity" and to celebrate it.'
– Pascale Petit

also by D. Nurkse

VOICES
over
WATER

D. Nurkse

CB *editions*

First published in the USA
in 1996 by Four Way Books
This edition first published in Great Britain in 2011
by CB editions
146 Percy Road London W12 9QL
www.cbeditions.com

Printed in England by Blissetts, London W3 8DH

ISBN 978-0-9561073-8-1

Voices over Water is the record of the lives of a married couple who emigrate from Estonia to Canada during the first half of the last century.

The woman, a preacher's daughter and musician from coastal Estonia, is the narrator for the first five poems of Part One, *Leaving Estonia*. Her husband's voice interweaves with hers for the rest of the section.

The man, an estate foreman, merchant and farmer, is the speaker in Part Two, *High Canada*.

The woman's voice returns as the major narrator in Part Three, *Easter Snow.*

Voices over Water is dedicated to Viktoria and Villem Nurkse. The events in this book are fictitious.

Contents

PART TWO · *High Canada*

PART THREE · *Easter Snow*

PART ONE

Leaving Estonia

The Nursery

I had only one bone button
but I had a hat with a plume
and a doll to command
made of a sack with eyes sewn on:
and each day when it was light
only in my mind, I played one game
I had played since I was born
and another I had never played before,
all by myself, wedged between brother and sister,
with the doll perched at my head and the infant
squirming at my feet, and that great chord of breath
drowning out the summer ocean.

The First Coast

We children came from anger.
On a calm night my parents
could elude each other, as if in a capital city,
in the hut with the bleached pine floor
between the gulf and the granite pastures.
Mother crushed myrtles between her fingers,
father picked at a knot with his teeth
or hummed the roots of A Mighty Fortress.
As soon as one of us could sing, she was assigned
lead soprano, and the other children
were pushed down to alto, tenor, baritone.
I was the eldest, I felt myself plummeting
down toward that bass-pedal pulsing
in my father's belly. I alone knew
that while he was harmonizing with all his strength
he was also listening, for an accidental, for a fox
in his bean patch, for a neighbor carousing
a mile across snow: he was a lay preacher
and once when we were walking he picked me up
and covered my eyes with his rabbitskin glove
so I crept back later and saw
a prostitute being pushed out to sea
in a boat with no oars. She was huge like my mother,
and even at seven I knew that one of the men
grunting on the dock must have been the lover,
but all wore frowns of innocence, all were certain
that not even God has responsibility
for the actions of the winter Baltic.

Island Music

When I skipped rope before memory
the song was already in my mouth
as the bread was hot on the table
and the sea cold behind the shutter.
I thought I was listening to the whistling rope
and to laughter and my breath, but I was hearing
a force unknowable as my body,
familiar as my father reading by his candle,
and the prayer that summoned this god was:
One And Two And Three And Four And.

*

One summer, the village elder pointed, saying
'don't waste money on a boy, whose voice will break.
Teach this one.' So they shipped me to land
and when I came back my girlfriends
were fat and angry and pledged to elders
and refused to speak to me: when I made my village debut
rain was drumming on the steeple and the audience
fell asleep as if I were delivering a sermon:
they woke long after I'd exhausted my repertoire,
stretching luxuriously, and only because the trade wind
was hammering at the black stained glass window

The Island Gospel

At fifty my father's strength
became savage and began to batter him
like breakers on a reef, strength against strength.
Though he could will himself to dream only of God's Love,
porcelain shattered in his grip.
He waved us children away as if we were smoke.
When he knew he was locked in his power
he stamped off to the store and bought a bolt
of black cloth for my mother, a new shovel
for my younger brother, and then he sat home
staring at a drawing of the sea, and his veins
swelled up like cable, and he wished in secret
there was another man strong as he on our island,
so he might kill instead of simply dying.

The Marriage to the Forest

When I took that farmer's ring I wrapped
my petticoats in my apron and moved inland.
The forest was no change: green all day,
blue by night, bowing and shivering
enough to make you sick: but if you tossed a stone
it sank without even flashing,
and nothing ever washed up on the edge.
Only once in forty years, a messenger
lost on the path from court to court
came stumbling out and whooped like an owl
when he saw us, then whispered
'at last I can breathe like a man
without that load of shadow.'
We explained this was just a clearing
with a hut, but he giggled and danced a hornpipe
on his bloated feet, so we bathed and fed him
but when we gave him directions
to the village four hours away
he just nodded and drooled, delirious
with joy at the lilt of our voices,
as if we were intoning scripture
and there was nothing to analyze,
so we made him a bed in the stable
and we nailed quilts over the green pine wall.

The Nine Owned Trees

This preacher's daughter claims to love me
in darkness and in church, and she can prove it
either way: she owns a calfskin book
and a dress made of tiny holes: she has
a sack of millet seeds, and perfect pitch,
and a swelling behind her cummerbund.
She doesn't know I was already in love
before she shared my bed, with those fruit trees
that I earned raking and burning
the landlord's leaves. I loved them best in winter
when I could see them all in one glance
no longer hidden by wind or each other,
as I could never see that woman
from start to finish, and best of all
they were mine clear, countersigned, paid for by sweat,
not by love, lies, happiness or suffering.

The Treaty Is Not Renewed

They warned us again and again
but we didn't believe it.
They were our masters, if they spoke
so clearly of war, we knew
in secret they must mean peace:
besides, how could any outcome
equal the horror of the omens?
We were tenants and had nothing
except our seed, and whatever crop
we could not move to market, animals
and a dog to watch them, and forty years
dreaming wide awake of an axe
about to fall a thousand miles away.

Slow Summer

The war was delayed, so was the truce
that would have concluded it,
the settling of the refugees
was postponed, and in that August
the frontier tangled like our bodies
in love, sometimes following
the river, sometimes swerving
inland across the vineyards
toward the shadow of the mountain
– then we moaned, not knowing
if we wanted a child
or to be free of each other
forever, and the apples
thickened till the branches bowed.

Factions

Horsemen came by my house
at night wanting to know
which side I was on.
At first I said: God:
meaning, nothing: but later
even that was not a safe answer.
I said the side of the poor
but that became very dangerous.
I explained that I was on the side
of God's poverty but not my own
and against the divinity of the poor
except in my case: but these were not men
given to subtleties: they had ridden hard
and their horses whinnied outside
lathered in the icy wind.

The Middle of the Forest

A crèche has been set up
at the crossroads, and above the infant,
right in the manger, the craftsman has placed
the figure of Jesus crucified, as if
night and day exist side by side
like two trees in the dim white forest:
but since noon I've been hearing drumming
and it's a soldier's drum: he might be practicing
or he might be transmitting orders, watching his own hands
become enchanted, become natural. I've smelled smoke
but it might be a charcoal burner in need
of Christmas money: all the same I wish
the drifting snow would hurry and blot out
the Star, the Kings, and the dying man.

The Rolls

The tax collector asked me
where I was from. I explained
'from this forest, sometimes
a little further in, sometimes
a little further out, but always
at the crossroads of two disused
logging paths, always with a springhouse,
always with my door facing south'
and he was amazed, being from a government
that had existed only a few days
and was bound to perish in a few hours.
He unpacked a roll of forms
and showed me where to enter
my intended harvest ten years from now
and who I was, and why I was not a traitor,
and the cost of each of my knives,
and I felt sorry for him, being forced
to beg from strangers, and yet
a peasant like myself, despite his tasselled shoes.

The Breached Frontier

A boy from our village enlisted.
Next year we glimpsed him
among the partisans, buying coal
along the forest margin, and the year after
we watched from a cellar chink
as he marched at the head of invading forces,
his eyes in vizor shadow, his lips smiling,
and we could remember him as a naked child
swinging on a village gate, watching
the summer clouds pour north.

Civil War

They set siege to a city
that had long ceased to exist,
that was only colonnades and lamps
softly guttering behind curtains, but they waited
for the population to surrender, though there was none,
the hands of the sentinel had turned to stone
around the rope to the white flag.
In another province, they bombed a city
with wire and nails, though it was theirs,
the women had divorced their husbands
to marry their children. They marched
through the orchards, forbidden to pick the fruit,
and if they chanced on a peasant milling cider
they hung him: they were invaders
but once they were our brothers, wailing
in the same crib, and it was then
that they hated us, now
we were just a problem to be solved.

A Letter from the Front

The thinness of the issue blankets
worn out by other bodies, living and dead,
reeking of them, soft where they were hard:
the meanness of the meals:
though my heart is full
when I say Grace, in my weakness
I gag at the hair, the sheen of sweat,
the bits of flies' wings, the spit
glinting on the surface of the tureen.
At night, the whine of bullets, as if
they could rest only in someone's head.
The deafness of the authorities.
Otherwise what kills me
is what always killed me,
my plantar's wart, the difficulty
of passing time without a clock
and washing without a mirror:
the memory of being punished
for stealing a candle my brother stole,
though I kept brave silence
and he made blushing denials:
the way they fastened the word Unlucky to me
before I had a chance to suffer.

Desertion

The enemy is so vast
they say if you burn your uniform
and forget who you were
you will find a house like yours
behind the lines, and children
like your brothers and sisters,
and you will find parents
who are missing a child
who looks like you, you will find lilac
in an alley and the smell of bread,
then you can rest and listen
to the drums of the reserve.

The Cock

A messenger knocked at our door
in parade dress, and announced
'the authorities know who you are
but as yet they have no reason to care.'
I told him to wait and my husband
ransacked our house for money,
finally he found a coin he'd hidden
in case of disaster and presented it
but the messenger stared at it
and said gravely: 'it hurts me to look
at a dead man's face,' so I begged him to wait
again while I ran to the yard
and chopped off a rooster's head,
and at last we watched the messenger disappear
into the thick of the forest, trailing
a thread of blood, with the claws running
in circles in the crook of the brocaded arm.

The Infiltration

The axe marks in the forest
filled with snow, clock faces
with no hands, and the hunters' trails
dovetailed with the quarry's.
At the center of the wilderness
hearth smoke shouted our coordinates
to the horizon, so we loved
in new positions, and planted
lilac in November, and turned the cow
to pasture among the cabbages, so that
the soldiers would not know us, as if
they had to know us to destroy us.

The Occupation

Once the professionals had killed each other
and the conscripts had deserted
the volunteers began to arrive: men who staggered,
eyes merry with wood alcohol,
and sometimes threw away their rifles
because the straps had chafed their shoulders.
We could have killed them, sometimes did,
but there were always more; it was futile
as standing in the rain to sponge the damp
off your old cow's back, or trying to fill out
any of the forms of any of our governments.
These new troops were certain they would die,
giggled over it, cared only about committing
enough crime so that God would not forget them
again in the next world: flies adored them:
even the scavengers who crept after them
barked orders at them: one time
they marched into the next village,
lined up all the livestock against a wall,
and executed them for violation
of an unannounced noon curfew, firing away
until even the hungriest of the scavengers
could only sell the scraps
for lead on the black market.
They came back, to our village, to apologize.
But by then we were just eyes in the forest,
whispers in an extinct language: we watched
from high in the trees as they dragged out
our old brocade dresses, and stuffed them with manure,

and bowed down to worship them: they broke down
our kitchen chairs for crucifixes:
they knelt in the snow and whipped themselves
with our expensive barbed wire, sobbing
God Have Mercy, and when they were seriously bleeding,
when their nude bodies turned sunset colors,
the sergeant slowly shook himself,
took a swig from a private flask,
hitched up his pants, puffed a cigarette
until he stopped shaking, and then barked:
'eyes right . . . eyes left . . . fall in . . .
attention . . . forward, march.'

Liberation

My husband was sentenced to the firing squad
and the poor came and prayed for him
saying: 'he was superintendent but so clumsy
at cards, he was almost one of us,
he was a moneylender at interest
but could never remember when it was compounded
and asked us for advice, though we were dying
of hunger, because those were the days
when we adored a painted God, like men
unable to fall asleep, before
the Revolution': and the new authorities
listened, bored, and granted the fool a new life.
Instead of coming home he took advantage
of Liberation to breed his favorite bitch
with one of the landlord's hunting dogs,
and he had to wait there, at the manor,
where it was death to be seen,
until the bitch had her morning sickness,
while he begged the passing troops
for a match for his cold pipe.
When he came home I'd been crying
a solid week, I thought he was resurrected
or just thrown back from death like a runt fish:
I said 'give me back my week of mourning
if you have the power to refuse heaven.'

The Marriage to War

I always expected my husband to leave me,
because he was the meekest man conceivable.
He sold his fruit trees for my singing lessons,
the quince for the major scales,
the plum for the minor,
then he had to barter his dusty flax
for my arpeggios, and to make weight
he hosed the consignment down.
They caught him and while he was in prison
I learned my first recitative
and all of an aria except one high note.
God knows what they did to him
but when he came back I sensed he blamed me.
He began signing contracts with vague salesmen
from countries that had already fallen,
shipping his contract timber by rivers
charted only in obsolete law books:
he was ruining himself slyly, as if with a whore,
but just when he was free, so deep in debt
he held the whole town in the grip of his weakness,
when his worst enemies prayed he would live forever,
the scouts began drifting in from the east.
They built a fire in our rose garden
and pounded on our door, demanding dry kindling.
They surfaced in the market on Sunday
and insisted on paying for every grain of barley
but the face on their coin was Satan's.
They were only the forerunners of the vanguard,
gorged on the endless dales of Karelia,

and what scared me was the camp followers
still a thousand miles behind; but I changed my mind
when I found a buck private hidden
in the coal bin, listening to my scales.
When I threatened him with the poker, he shook himself
like a dog and whispered: Do Re Mi, Mi Re Do,
as if it were a language: then I knew it was time.
I caught my husband as he was drifting out the door,
flat paper roses in his pocket, claiming
he was on his way to feed the pond carp,
and I forced him to load our wagon
with the chest of old love letters, the washboard,
the metronome and a change of linen.
Looking back an hour later, my husband pointed
to a small white cloud and said: 'that's our house,
if it were wet smoke from green forest wood
it would have hung in the wind a few seconds longer.'

Rumors

We halted in a village a day's march from the sea.
All my husband could talk about
was things we'd forgotten: the oak bucket,
the shadowbox, the dog's comb that had a scrolled clasp.
I told him these things can be found in other worlds,
but he trembled and counted up their virtues,
innumerable as the strengths of the dead, though they still
    existed
and could have been picked up and fitted on the cart
if only we'd remembered the child's sleigh and the hemp
    rope.
He rocked in his sleep moaning the names
of his hunting boots, that had middle- and nicknames,
and next dawn the rumors began

            and wove themselves around us in a net of voices
speaking authoritatively whether we slept or woke.
It was hard to know where they came from
since there was no one left on the streets
except a blind inn owner, three little girls,
a cat, and an old man whose wife's cousin
had once studied Morse: but the rumors intensified
until our footsteps and the baby's breath and the squeak
of our frozen cuffs against our wrists all sounded
like speech: and the rumors were of peace,

            our masters had met in an unknown city
with their bankers and clerks and killers and priests
all disguised as farmers, all carrying sacks of seed,
and they'd signed a document in code swearing
not to burn each other. To us the war was already old,

tinged with the sweetness of a childhood nightmare,
but the gossip mounted with every breath
like a shutter banging in the wind. The innkeeper
groped around with pitchers of pressed flowers
to cheer the guests who were certain to return,
the girls braided victory wreaths
to sell to any of the soldiers of any of the armies,
the cat rubbed against our legs: next night
we could not sleep for the rumors flying between us,
pounding in our ears: next day we began to retrace our steps
back towards the farm but there were still fires on the horizon
and dazed men walking in the opposite direction.
When we asked them for news they blinked
as if waking from a deep sleep and asked in return
            – which way is the ocean?

The Hidden Fighters

We retraced our steps though the signs were bad.
At twilight a huge man stood in the road with an axe
and when he saw us he whimpered in terror and plunged
    into the undergrowth
though we were just two peasants, a child, and a deaf horse.
At night we found our moonlit road
obstructed by wheels: wheels of carts, phaetons,
coaches, surreys, toy horses, all frozen.
So we drifted along by the logging paths
that were sometimes just accident, angles of snow and
    windbreak.
Sunrise was black because we were so deep,
the rustle of the owls stopped,
we came upon a child's swing dangling from a branch
and then another and another, a forest of swings.
We found a glass case covered with branches:
it contained an encyclopedia. Then we looked up
and saw the carcasses of butchered deer
lashed to the treetops and painted chalk white
like enormous clumps of snow and we knew
we were in the camp of the partisans
and the silence around us was not ours,
nor was it the silence of fear.

Spies

When we stepped into the clearing
the officers arrested us.
They told us we were pretending
to be afraid, to be homeless,
to be nameless.
They stripped us of disguises.
They shot our horse.
They made us swear we were spies
by the blood of Jesus, by our mothers' eyes,
by the smell of bread and mown grass,
by the murmur of a child asleep.
Then they took us to their fortress.

Expulsion

They asked our names, if we were married,
and who were we? They allowed us
to answer the last question with the first two.
Under our breath we were rehearsing, No,
we do not sympathize with the Revolution,
the counterrevolution, God, Satan
or atheism: but they did not ask,
they spared us.
                    It was almost cruel.
Then we stood in the stunning cold
to wait for our visas, in that crowd
of ministers, peddlers, bankers,
judges, thieves, and nuns,
huddled outside the garrison door.

PART TWO

High Canada

The New World

The dogs barked, but not just at me:
at all the strangers lined up on the wharf,
some in frock coats and some in denim.
Once, the foreman came out and pointed
at one of us who wore a leather apron:
otherwise dusk fell and the baying of the hounds
forgot us and became ecstatic and sorrowful
and the tiny windows of the granaries they were guarding
held the sun and darkened: the wind rose: at night
the foreman's daughter tiptoed out and asked us
what we wanted and we said politely
in all our languages or in mime
Work: and she answered politely
that she could give us bread and even meat
in charity, or a night's rest, as for work
she was just a child and had hardly enough
to tide herself till daybreak.

A Window in Saskatoon

We lurch side by side
in a dance to no music,
staring through that reflection
at a darkness hard as flint:
sometimes a lamp wavers:
it seems impossible
that a world could be large as this night:
then a shower of sparks
is thrown in our face
harmlessly, another station,
and my wife hunts for a clock
that will show her our lateness,
but what I long to see
is one more smoldering hearth
with a row of lit books,
volume on volume of bound past,
since I never had her schooling.

Plains

In this country there's a thousand miles
between one milestone and the next.
The wells are so deep you drop a bucket
and lace your boots before it hits water.
Sometimes you see the smoke and lights
of a huge city on the skyline
and you know it's the herd being ridden south:
then the ground shakes for days
but you hear nothing except prairie dogs
bickering over stones: and this silence
is like a strong arm encircling my wife,
protecting her from those strangers
who once were the world.

The Eye of Winter

In the forerunner of the blizzard, my neighbor
lashed himself to his doorpost and went out
to mind a colicky sheep but the rope froze
stiff as a poker and his hands froze to it:
he was held like a figure on a weathervane
or meat on a spit, out into nothing.
When the storm itself came I battened my windows.
The wind was like nothing that had ever happened
or could happen, in me and outside,
there was delight in that voiceless calling,
so I filled my mind with the cleanup chores
I would have to do but they became brief
as matches, my dreams were no shelter,
even the absence of all my dead
was blown away. Then the calm came.
I stepped toward the door.
My wife threw a cup of coffee in my face,
she hit me with a shovel, and I didn't even turn,
just stood there staring
at that quivering doorknob as if
it was the door that had stunned me.

Sea of Grass

I'm nothing without my weariness.
Last night I slept eight hours
and my children hardly recognize me,
my wife blinks. I saddle my stallion
and when I order Git without stammering
or lurching, he puts his head down and resumes
grazing his portion of the infinite prairie.

A Year of Hunger

When the famine came
we ate our seed, our horsefodder,
our chickenfeed, our broody hens,
our milk cow, and then we ate
dust and slugs and hoarded sugar.
We became weak and dizzy and saw
God too easily, in every shift of wind.
At last a neighbor came riding
with a city paper announcing
in banner type: FAMINE ENDS.
We saw it was dated a week ago
and a new prosperity was spreading
north with the ground thaw,
the value of land was shooting up
all around us, and that night
we killed the stud bull,
toasted our luck in his blood,
broke a winestem, made love,
woke at noon and suddenly
began waiting.

The Market Holds

We've hoarded our delights
like pennies in a sock
and they're heavy: our children
cry from dreams not hunger.
We weep for those we left behind
to die in our place, our fathers
and sisters, but we also understand
our horse is paid for, and the front wheels
of the buggy, and seven spokes in the rear:
the pots in the kitchen, though not the lids:
the curtains, though not as yet
the velvet ropes that hold them open
so that all who pass may know
we're still in love, we work, we lack nothing.

Precious Dust

She wants a porcelain jug
to pour milk, while metal
was good enough for my mother:
still I hitch my cart and bargain
with that beaming merchant and stow the package
among my new coping-saw blades,
exactly like my father's but twice as sharp.
I drive home along the goat-path,
ambling between the fence-lines, and present her
with the chips and the china dust, saying
don't lose a fragment, no matter how small.

Shared Land

I'm caught like a fish in my work.
Each gesture pulls the mesh tight: my land
is staked, mapped, ploughed, taxed,
but certain papers are missing, a few drops
of vaccine that would have saved a sick colt
trickled out, the axle is working loose
under the wagon that carries my children to church:
there are gaps in my fence, if the herd finds them
they will trample my house and the fault
will be mine in the judge's eyes. If I'd hoarded
my silver change from the dead world
I could buy stretched wire and willing labor,
but it was spent on buttons and thread.
All day I've been splitting kindling
in the front yard, and my flagstones
still lead to my door, my smoke
plumes above my chimney, but it's all
a mirage without the next axe-blow
                and whenever I catch my breath
my wife sweeping indoors resumes
her one aria, in that old determination
to get through the music and back
to the silence of a clean kitchen, and her routine
disgusts me, as I chop I mutter
her name again and again as if
praying to a god seen every night.

The Well

Am I rich or poor? I tilled one furrow
until the horse dropped, but the wind erased it.
I had to find my way home by Polaris.
All that grew was wasted time, each speck of dust
ripened to a cloud: it took a year
to strike water. I shouted upwards
at a smaller smaller square of sky until at last
I raised my hands from the clay and tasted dew
from the center of the earth. I threw away my shovel,
galloped to the church and knelt and praised God
in the throng of worshippers, some begging for mercy,
some mouthing the parable of the eye of the needle,
some watching their neighbors through cupped hands.

Increase

A good harvest means bad luck.
A wife who'll cry when you're hurt
means no luck. Worst of all,
a baby laughing when you come home
means nine lives of misfortune.
I learned this when I was a manchild
in the old world, when I was just
a shriek in a crib, before they taught me
'all things come to the one who waits.'

The Years of Fine Harvest

I can still split fence rail all day
and the same night read from Thessalonians to Jude
without blinking or moving my lips,
and then wake before dawn to nurse a whimpering lamb
whose bellow I would have slept through.
I can still resist the temptation
to see myself as strong; my neighbors
can do more and my rulers can do nothing.
In August when the plains are white to harvest
I yearn to leave the grain to rot
and it isn't fear of famine that makes me reap
but just the bias towards a known miracle.
Then the assessor comes to prod my packed barn
and I itch to take a knife and cross the gap
between my debts and his deficit: and he laughs
and pats my shoulder, knowing
if I long to I will not.

Desirable Land

One good harvest and the neighbors are jealous.
If not, they should be, all I had when I came
was the habit of never sleeping.
Now I'm at the mercy of any newcomer
who might toss a dead cat in my well.
All night I hide in my long grasses
watching for a man's shadow, as I once kept vigil
for rain clouds: but there are only the shadows
of the owls that multiplied in the snowless spring,
gliding on earth like black feather dusters pulled
by long invisible strings, not really trespassers
unless the price of grain goes even higher.

Lost Lamb

I went looking for the cry from the fog
and suddenly I was gone. I took out my compass
but couldn't see the letter N. I struck a match
and saw no flame. I had to kneel
and grope with my ungloved hand, until I sensed
the void of my bootprint, and even there
I touched fog thick as frayed felt.
On hands and knees I groveled
from emptiness to emptiness until I banged my head
against my kitchen step. When I opened my door
my wife and children were lined up on the sofa,
giggling at a drawing I did as a child,
preserved in a musty album. I said nothing
but marched to the screened corner and filled
the oak tub with kettle water, feeling that blank
in my pupils and nostrils and eardrums.
I scrubbed and scrubbed, and that night
I slept with a flickering candle, but my dreams
of the other world are still terrifyingly clear.

The Shy One

My wife grows foreign as if
each night we pumped
distance from the well:
while the girl I never married
conquers her awe and raps
on my glass at dawn,
trembling in that village lace
of fifty years ago, in her hair
a drifted leaf and a silver comb.

The Year in Bed

I'm inhabited like a house
but the tenant's just an idea, a few degrees
of heat, and can't even be pinned down
to misfortune: I'm forced to sweat, the only cure
for this presentiment that's made me old.
Eight months and they've pushed my bed
close to the window and propped it up
since the snow reaches halfway up the glass.
Now I can watch the glare, the cloud empire,
my old dog suddenly at eye level, coat
sleek with wind, puppyish
with distance, as he sniffs out
the gates in the buried fences.

In Sickness

I dreamt I sailed home
and opened my door, when I woke
I had fever: suave as a lover's touch,
then a meticulous fiancée, at last
a wife who ruled me. The cry on my lips
repeats of its own accord and the thoughts
in my brain dress and groom each other,
explaining that my children have plotted
to kill me and feed me to the hogs:
that the land bank offered them work:
that my body is just a gauze curtain
twitching in front of rage:
that the distance between my hand
and the night glass is greater than the journey
from my tiny country to this unmade bed.

Snowbound

My sickroom is also the pantry
the linen closet and the smithy
so I fix my eyes on my silent window.
December climbs to the top of the sash,
the sky thickens and darkens like kneaded batter.
The drifts are mountains without maps, fantastic
but not imaginary, not permanent. All day
sparks from the anvil glisten over me,
or my children's tears, but I no longer
need to die, I could live forever
in this blue womb where shadows
march behind aging light and my breath
whirls up the chimney like smoke. Our words
have died so we each work or sleep
in perfect balance with the inner enemy,
and that will to erase all obstacles,
that once crippled me, has grown bland
in this house whose doors
buckle in a wind I cannot feel.

The Cure

I rose and it was finished.
My bed was soaked as if a spring had gushed up:
the imprint of my body glittered, rippled, and faded
    smooth.
I staggered to the door and rapped.
My knuckle stung: I was no longer
shielded by that mantle of pain.
No one was home. Framed in my window I'd watched
faces in passing clouds: lovers, soldiers, fathers:
but in my open doorway, range after range
of nothing sailed south,
and the harsh song of starlings
was amplified by light snow.
I limped to my toolshed and found
my mattocks and hoes shod with green rust,
but the shafts were polished
to radiance by strangers' use.

Foot Soldiers

Every night the ones who died
come to me and show me their wounds.
They indicate I am unmarked
and besides, am living,
though once I suffered beside them.
They irritate me, having no legitimate claim
except that of being forgotten
in a forgotten war, between governments
long since toppled by internal enemies.

The Testament

I don't want to be so rich
my children depend on me, or so poor
I'm a burden, therefore
I have irrigated land and strong enemies.
I don't want to be so loved
that my death will destroy my house.
I want to be remembered for what I gave away,
not what I built. Let my neighbors mourn
the appointed span, not a second more.
My wife's remarrying must be to a stranger.
I want the preacher to read the exact words
that were spoken over my father and grandfather
– Blessed be the barren tree that gives no fruit.
I want the gravediggers to be paid in copper
and go home satisfied but not embarrassed.

The Stone Boat

Two fingers under topsoil we hit granite.
The land was empty to the horizon
and perhaps if we'd kept walking
we would have found moist yielding earth,
but we had to cleave to our own
because it had been freely given us:
then all summer we labored loading
the sleigh with stones and dragging it
behind borrowed oxen, to build a sheep pen.
Now twenty years later the stone boat is dust,
but I dream I'm yoked to it naked
and when I wake my wife and I make love
for the first time since I was given last rites,
and we lie together breathing lightly, wasting
minutes of sleep precious as bushels of wheat,
and we listen as each oak stair creaks at its joint
and each strut and pin moans in turn.

PART THREE

Easter Snow

Building on Rock

All summer we stretched the foundation lines
so tight we felt our pulses throb: then we dug:
we opened the sealed earth with crowbars and ballpeen
   hammers,
assembled our roof and at last framed our walls,
the windows mitred gaps in a grid of gaps,
and at every delay my husband thought of winter
but every time he cut his finger
or a chigger bite became infected
he remembered God, the Lord of Hosts,
and looked up at the clouds, or the countless stars,
muttering praise in his dead language.

A Song of Exile

The villagers fuss in Sunday clothes on Saturday,
clutching their shiny knees. The eldest commands me:
Sing. I dust off my portrait of Brahms
and adjust the lectern. With shaking hands
I set the metronome, fast like a bird's heart,
slow like a riderless horse at a funeral,
slow like a listener's heartbeat, fast
like a performer's. I say: that's what music is,
but they sense I'm stalling so I count my entrance.
I count the doves in my grandfather's oak
that I saw with a child's eyes, I count the agates
my husband gave me, that I smuggled in a straw hat
past the German guards at Tartu, then I open my mouth
and the voice comes out and it is monstrous:
part squawk, part labor moan, more imperious
than my own forgotten bitterness, floating
like a huge ghost between me and my neighbors.
I try to coax it up a half tone
and it soars to the ceiling, I try to bring it down
and it sinks with a crash: finally
I just starve it of breath, and it is silence,
midsummer, Western Canada, and I say:
that was a *lied* by Brahms. They shuffle and mutter
and say out loud: not like the songs we get on the radio
on Sundays in clear weather. I agree
serenely, so that they shake my hand
dubiously, and one of them kisses it
equally dubiously, and walking that night
in the dark streets, sometimes I hear

a caterwaul from a shuttered window, or a grim hiccup
followed by applause, but when I get home
all I do is cry, for the first time in their language.

Cold Brahms

I dusted my book of *lieder* with a feather.
It was gray with fungi, glued shut
by cat vomit, and I prized it open
with tweezers in case my rough hands
might pulverize it. I set it
on a music stand made of chicken coops
and thought how hard it would be and choose
to think how easy it might be
and made myself silent and went
to empty my bowels and looked out the window
and saw the quarter note crows
perched on the telegraph wire,
and one half note snowy falcon
waiting: and beyond them
the same blank shimmer over the Great Slave Lake,
the Great Bear Lake and the summits
of the Chenang mountains, where diamonds
crack with cold in the valleys, and beyond that
the Arctic where ice shifts
at the rate of an inch a century,
and then Russia and the education colonies.
I cleared my throat and tried to put
all this information into the first note:
it was *Mi Bemol* and came out
a little clearer than I expected, but I knew
it would take me years to relearn even the first measure
so I cursed out loud and then appealed to God,
but my daughter consoled me, pointing out
this was Canada, there were no Cossacks,

no Germans, no village drunks with guns
and principles, no elders with prize cattle
to die for, nothing
in fact, except that telegraph line
linking frozen seas: so that I might live
as long as I had to.

Mistakes

The complicated passages I master without effort.
I learned the trills and semiquavers listening
to my son's intricate breathing when he was so cold,
newborn in the withered forest. But at the simple
long held notes my mind falls asleep as I taught it to
when anything is prolonged, as it slips into a trance
when the feed falls towards the chickens or the broom
inches toward the pan or sweat glides after fever,
and I drop right back into the old bitter dream
that began in my mother's womb, as if
now were my chance to master my illusion
of always dying, and when I look up
the pianist is staring at me baffled:
I used to swing my fan and stare back
disdainfully, but I've had to train myself
to blush, because he's the only sober maestro
between these plains and the Great Slave Lake.

Equinox

Every day I scrubbed the house,
but every spring I chiselled it
out of carbolic, lye, fire, ammonia,
pear vinegar, lunar caustic and muriatic acid
with wirebrushes and holland paper,
and that night if my husband came near me
I turned to the wall for it was my one chance
to sleep without dreams, before the wind
veers south and flowers open overnight.

No Harvest

Anything my husband owns
becomes his manhood: his wheat,
his dog, the shadow of a cloud
the instant it passes over
his stake, a fly buzzing
at the inner perimeter of his doorway:
his manhood weighs on me:
and the drought in the next province
is so savage, the sky is black
with smoke from precautionary fires.

The Human Chain

My husband stands in line
and whenever a swung bucket spills
he sighs: the water is his
while the smoldering barn has been ruled
collateral on a huge debt.
If he's handed one of his oak buckets
he just holds it in both hands murmuring
Thank You . . . but if it's a neighbor's pail
he'll pass it on to the fire fighter
in the glinting asbestos mask.

The Oak Bed

The wedding sheet frayed under us
so I cut it in four and sewed it back
with the unworn edges at the center,
and when that center became transparent
I cut on the diagonal and sewed it back
matching worn cloth with worn cloth
until I had a mackerel sky of diamond rags,
degrees of use, and still each night
we'd sit at the edge of the mattress
trembling with exhaustion and at last turn
as if unwed, to that silence between us.

The Summons

I heard the dog howling
from that grove of nine dwarf trees
my husband was trying to nurse.
As I came close, the high cold throat-note
began to resonate in my copper earrings
and all at once I was reassured
seeing it was a trick being played
with a wild animal and a dead body
and I knew my husband was behind it –
I looked for him beyond the withered trunks
hardly wide enough to conceal their own shadows,
but I knew it was his idea and not a neighbor's
because the prop was dressed in his coat,
                              and wore his smile
and his blood had frozen under it.

The Last Preparation

The preacher's daughter came to lay the body out
and I stood beside her wondering if I dared
pay for her labor, until the silver burnt
with cold in my palm: but she flushed,
then sweated with the effort of coaxing him from his trance,
working the corners of the mouth up and pummeling
the eyelids down over that streaked void, even though
I'd wheeled him into the sun three noons running.
When she was gone, accepting nothing, I saw she'd prodded
his limbs into prayer, but to me it looked
like two wrestlers' hands locked in a game
and I knew the right was stronger
so I leaned a little on the left:
then I washed my body and waited indoors
for the footfall of the comforters' horses
plodding on their glass-smooth road.

The Body Across the Yard

The children keep tugging at my skirts
and asking: who killed him? and I say
no one. He's laid out in the barn
until the earth thaws, and at first
the candle burned steady
at his right hand, but in midwinter
it began to gutter out in draughts,
and one night I forgot to light it, and the next
I needed matches for the stove, and the third night
the flint was worn smooth: then I was shaken
awake before dawn by the idea of that darkness
unimaginable as the night under my own skin
                         and tiptoed out
 and the owl was perched can the barn gable
with its cat-face and eyes like gold coins.

Funeral Feast

When he died I was dated
as if I were the one whacked into marble
with a mallet and chisel.
You could run your fingers over me, I was
the surface of his deep-veined name.
Instead of a woman I'd become
the idea of contained suffering, a bitch
chasing its tail in praise
of Lazarus. I had to sit
with the other widows: all they talked about
was their husbands' bad habits:
mine had so many I had nowhere to begin.
I sat mute, making a tilled field
in the mashed potatoes, a dam of gravy,
the peas were tiny Orthodox churches,
a carrot slice was a synagogue,
corn was Rome all lit at midnight,
the broccoli a forest where we Lutherans
pray without confessional: then my plate
was empty, and I was still hemmed in
by widows, creatures with time to burn.

Limbo

Come Sunday, we're inoculated
with a dose of future disaster
as the preacher in his groomed voice
catalogues the Lake of Fire:
but my catastrophe is in the past,
so is my work, my death
is just a weekday habit
like plucking a chicken or tossing
a tress whenever I pass my mirror
– and I think it would be too cruel
to pay God back
in His coin, in suffering.

Surviving Partner

Satan tempted me
to his paradise of despair,
explaining that no one
would ever fathom my grief.
I refuted him, pointing out
that this world is full of widows,
broken cups and cracked mirrors,
and that the body propped in the barn
had been a cheating husband,
a man like the rest, not saved
or damned. I was so stubborn
Lucifer grew afraid and left,
then my enemy was God's mercy
poured out second after second.

Buried Stone

When the graveyard is covered with snow
the minister hitches up his plough
and cuts a road into it.
He consults a chart, and shows us mourners
where to kneel along that blinding drift.
Then I force my mind to picture
the chiselled name, date, and legend
HUSBAND OF, followed by that lovingly polished blank.

The Knots

Widows visit and tell me
'he's resting' or they claim
'he's in paradise': at first
I thought these were conflicting schools
and there'd be resolution, but now
I hear both on the lips of the same guest:
'rest = paradise, paradise = rest,'
with no change in the tight down-forced smile,
though they all know as well as I do
that all that ever kept my husband going
was having one knot to tie
and another to undo, without his two knots
he would have vanished even in life
and been forgotten forever.

The Frayed Veil

Now he's gone
I want a divorce.
We each had our faction.
Mine scattered when his heart stopped,
as if hunted by a secret police:
his followers grow fresh
and smirk their grief in my face.
All night, his horse
stamps in my stable.
Even the pastor, my oldest ally,
now takes his side and says:
Let the Dead Bury the Dead.

Afterlife

I heard the hens squawking
but I was too tired
to go pick up the laying.
Next dusk I heard
the cat stepping on the eggs: by then
the cow was bellowing to be milked
but I lay with this tiredness
the exact length of my body, pressing
on top of me like a lover
with a slow meticulous hand
and I had cheated on my husband
though he was dead and had no one
or, knowing him, everyone
to sleep with in return.

Writing Home

Sometimes I feel blessed, sometimes
all I can remember is a passing cloud,
a bee in the doorway, dust
caked on the roof of my mouth: then I sit straight
and write myself a letter, in scrolled cursive,
solicitous of health and family, and blot it.
I button my Sunday dress and tie the fringed umbrella
to the buggy, against the dust, and drive to the box.
When I come back I blow gently on my cold tea:
since I'm so tired, and so far from the center,
it may take a lifetime for the news to arrive.

The Draft

March blows the seeds I scatter
back in the folds of my black fringed shawl.
At dusk I read the Bible but when I put it down
the pages turn of their own accord
from Kings to Revelations, and wherever
I sit I am cold, facing
the north like a mirror with no features,
and my hair drifts across my brow as if fingers
were running through it, but the gesture has a name:
March: and my mind wanders.
I think of Zion, the City of God,
that my people once planned to die to build.
I wonder if the smoke hangs level
as the horizon over the chimneys there,
if the clouds there pass at such speed
that every day seems long and short
as the two thousand years since crucifixion,
and whether all the golden shutters
are banging across the black diamond windows.

Tracks

I woke and found one set of footsteps
frozen in spring mud, leading to the horizon.
My children were asleep and my man long buried:
I guessed a prowler had scudded out
over crusted snow, and escaped at dawn.
I learned to keep my house shuttered
and to sleep with an awl: then I overheard
my children whispering that I'd lost my soul,
that I was more loving as a picture in a book
than as a widow guarded by spring rain.

Wind Thieves

They know exactly what they want
and where to find it: one comes for the china,
one for the silver, one for the braided wig,
one for the foxtail coat, and they leave their big jute sack
outside, weighted with a stone, but they never finish
because something terrifies them: perhaps the noise I make
trying to strike the flint against the wick
of that sputtering lamp propped
where my husband used to lie.

The Old Profile

When the day circled on the calendar dawned
I boiled my mourning clothes in the tub
till the dye bled and they were gray.
I scrubbed them, and aired them
for three windy nights, and folded them
along lines delicate as tracks in new snow,
transparencies established by a lifetime
of waiting in the back of a drawer, and replaced them
in the cedar chest beside the smudged diploma,
the dark blue curtain that cannot endure sunlight,
and the silhouette they cut of me as a bride
with real holes in paper lace, making me sit still
for an hour that seemed a thousand years.

Locusts

First I heard a scissors snipping velvet, then the clip
as the shears travel on in midair, then singing
from everywhere, from my own throat, but no bass note.
When I opened my honey jar I felt the first
soft explosion and the tiny legs mounted up
under the door. I took my pepper mill and ground them
for sacks of fertilizer, but the jute disappeared
and there were just clumps of minced eyes
following me: then they flew away. I had to chop
my lace dresses for doilies and sew bandannas
into my foxtail coat. I waited six days, and counted out noon
by the hourglass, and put on my second-best veil
swathed in muslin, so as not to choke
on minute feelers. I tacked to the road where the postman's
orange lantern was yawing and luffing. I shouted,
shouted, and his shadow mimed an answer, he pressed
his goggles against my mouth and I asked: is this a plague?
And he answered: no; it all happened before.
Then he gave me a letter and when I was home
I scraped off the glinting film of eggs
and found it was from my sister in the other world,
whom I hadn't seen since childhood: she told me
she was still being spared, and asked for a spool, a needle,
a thimble, a nib, and a clean blank envelope.

Extinction

That fall the wild pigeons passed over us.
I woke and there was a river in the sky and a black
sunset that lasted until nightfall.
They settled on the shrub I planted
in memory of my husband's fruit trees
until it broke under them. They nestled on the scarecrow
and stained it solid as a statue with their droppings,
they gathered on the roof and eaves and ledges
and doorknobs and filled the house with a pulsing
as of a great heart outside the body. I fell on my knees
and prayed: can there be another war more bitter
than the one that destroyed us long ago?
The next day there was no dawn and I knew
this was more than an omen and asked God:
can there be a world more hidden than this one,
sparser, emptier, that they are escaping to?
That night there was no nightfall but next day
they were gone and their droppings
had frozen in little walls, like the foundations
of a city still to be built.

Unheard Music

I believe in my strength
or in the dregs of my strength: dying I
no longer have to split these hairs: dying I
no longer need to rise to the challenge
of every lost stranger, every unfinished thought,
every wind playing in shadow branches.
Let them follow me, if they want to know
what breath tastes of. I at my leisure
close my eyes and practice my aria.
I imagine a beautiful woman singing
and when the sorrow becomes too much, I stop
and let the music close at its own pace.

The Wake

Dozing, I saw a file of old women
in frozen veils, padding through the snow,
pushing wheelbarrows of mortar
or tottering under hods: in the sky
the scaffolding for the tower loomed,
and I was a little girl watching: then I dreamt
my parents were rocking my crib and whispering
that I must wake, the snow has died down
and the north wind has fallen silent.

The Return to the Stage

I feel like a ghost, leaving this house
in which I buried my husband, two sons,
and a father's memory: under my corset
I carry my scores, and I sense those black quarter notes
swarm over my skin like beetles: I'm going to sing
and die in the endless city, in front of lights
and a raised curtain, my ears ringing
with laughter or boos or silence,
not like my father who died
at home behind nailed shutters, annihilated
by slighted pride.

Arrival in the City

It starts to rain at the bridge
and by the nineteenth bridge
the rain has turned to snow.
When the Greyhound stops at the lights
there's an empty moment.
She thinks: in a city this big
how will my own death find me?

And if you find me how will you know me
from the other women with parcels
and visas with faded stamps,
snowbound in buses
while the wind whips on the roofs?

Then the lights stop changing
behind a wall of brilliant vagueness
and she's neither traveling nor standing still.
She permits herself a brief dream
in which she allows nothing to happen
and when she wakes
they've passed Naptown, Fishburg, Lamp Hill,
and stopped at the corner of Ninetieth and Tenth
and the tenement is larger than any palace.

She composes herself
in the sour box of the elevator
and starts down the corridor.

Each door has a little number
or a numbershaped absence where the tin was stolen

and she smells kielbasa platanos marijuana and lye:
then she hears the music: polka merengue breakdown
gavotte delta blues cumbia, a phone ringing
on a radio, a phone in a room where a sleeper
is dreaming, a phone in an empty room, a phone
ringing while whoever might answer is busy
peering out the keyhole, and back to fado
sarabande Charleston plainchant hornpipe:
she opens the one door her key will fit
and enters silence.

Grandmother's Cold

All her life she'd groomed herself
for the needle's eye.
But when she was dying
she cried out
Who is this dying?
She asked me to turn
the portraits to face the wall
so she could admire their blank backs
stamped with blurred serial numbers
or patents of village artists.
She forced me to dismantle
the heirloom clock, so she might
touch the promised jewels
and see if her swollen fingers
could turn the tiny disconnected wheels. . . .
She asked me to open the Bible
and read a verse at random
and when I did, she cursed me
and made me try again
until I found one that made sense.
Then she cleared her throat, rolled over,
and reminded me to put her eiderdown
in cold storage, and buy rouge,
eyeshadow, and cut-rate
wine for the professional mourners.

Inventing Nations

My grandmother's flesh has grown luminous,
cloudy behind her nylon housecoat.
Since her treatments, she can keep down
only jello, sherry, and whipped cream.
She stays up all night watching old movies:
sometimes she loses her temper, turns off the sound,
and hexes the characters in a language
no one in this city has heard of: by day
she stares at the Hudson framed in her window.
She can no longer identify the flags of freighters
and asks me to, but strain as I may
my vision blurs, and she insists, so I wind up
inventing nations: Liguria, Phoenicia,
Babylonia . . . and she nods. On her wall
Kennedy faces Truman but there's no picture
of the child dead of consumption
or the child dead of hunger
or the child who was my father
who succeeded, whose heart failed:
all there is from that world is a locket
showing the infant Mozart playing silence
on a tiny clavichord, behind cracked glass.

Ⓑ editions

www.cbeditions.com